Getting through What You Are Going Through

A Guide to Dealing with Trouble in a
Practical and Biblical Way

To King & Latonia
Many blessings to you.
Ernest W. Jones, Ph.D.

Ernest W. Jones

ISBN 978-1-0980-0539-9 (paperback)
ISBN 978-1-0980-0540-5 (digital)

Christian Faith Publishing, Inc.
832 Park Avenue
Meadville, PA 16335
www.christianfaithpublishing.com

Scripture quotations labeled KJV are from the King James Version of the Bible.

Scripture quotations labeled NLT are from the Holy Bible, New Living Translation, copyright © 1996, 2004, 2007 by Tyndale House Foundation. Used by permission of Tyndale House Publishers, Inc., Carol Stream, Illinois 60188. All rights reserved.

Printed in the United States of America

Acknowledgements

I am indebted to the many who encourage me to fulfill God's purpose for creating me. It begins with my wife Cynthia, who believes in me and provides the necessary prayer covering for all I do. My daughter Jessica, who inspires me everyday without fail. To the many spiritual leaders that I have been privileged to serve under, I pray this book measures up to the invaluable teaching you have deposited into my life. And finally, I acknowledge the awesome group of believers I shepherd at True Vine Ministries. Your belief in me consistently makes me want to do amazing things for God.

Contents

Introduction

The *purpose* of this book is to help us all to deal with the various things that we have to go through.

Going through is a part of everyone's life; it is a part of the package of life and we should all be aware of this. This book is being shared to supply us as believers a strategy to "get through whatever we have to go through" in the most godly and responsible way possible.

Unfortunately, in a lot of our preaching delivered from our westernized pulpits we don't hear *how to go through* messages because we are always guaranteed instant deliverance or an "at midnight" deliverance. I am in no way against the message, but what happens if what we are dealing with in life doesn't expire at midnight? What if we don't get the instant miracle? What if we pray three times for the thorn to be removed from our flesh and nothing happens? What are we to do? What are we to think? This is the teaching that is missing.

As a student of history, I could make a laundry list of believers from antiquity who were tortured, imprisoned, and treated horribly for their faith. We are not better Christians than they were. These people were committed believers, yet they went through. Hence, we will have to go through as well.

Therefore, if you are going through right now, I want this book to coach you through it. I want what you read to build your faith and connect you to the God who is in control of all things! Or maybe you are not going through right now, but you know someone who is, and we all do. My prayer is that the nuggets on these pages help you to help someone else.

Now let's get started on this journey.

Everyone Goes Through

I t has been rightly said, "Into each life some rain must fall." Well, actually it was a song. It was in 1944 that The Ink Spots,[1] along with Ella Fitzgerald, went to the top of the charts with the song of this title.

There is much truth to these sentiments. Each of us will experience some loss, some disappointment, some setback, some "rain" that we are going to have to deal with as we live here on this earth. These things are unavoidable; we have to go through them.

Let's define what we mean by "going through."

Going through, simply put, is to undergo a difficult or painful period or experience according to the dictionary. This period may last for a day, a week, or even years as painful as that is to share with you. Yep, I want weeping to endure for one night, and joy to come in the morning just like you, but that is not what happens in reality to many of us.

Did you not know that the Bible warns God's people that there should be an expectation of trouble at any moment of life? Two major scriptures stick out: one from the Old Testament and one from the New Testament.

In the book of Job, there is a piece of reality written there that should sober us from any fairy tale of living. In chapter 14, verse 14 (KJV), it is recorded, "Man that is born of a woman is of few days and full of trouble." Pretty shocking, huh?

[1.] https://en.wikipedia.org/wiki/The_Ink_Spots.

This scripture covers us all. We are all born of a woman. Now my real deep friends will twist this truth by saying, "Well, that's a BC scripture." Meaning, a before-Christ scripture, and that once we are *born again*, it does not apply. Oh, how I wish this was true.

When we become born again, we don't cease being human and experiencing human events. We still come face-to-face with troubles and problems and calamities and situations and circumstances and on and on.

The benefit of being born again is that we go through these events with God's help. Being born again empowers us to confront and survive earthly perils. Now let's see what is being said in the New Testament that gives us a signal that maybe we should expect to go through some things.

The scripture I desire to allude to comes from the pen of the apostle Peter. Peter writes, "Beloved, think it not strange concerning the fiery trial which is to try you, as though some strange thing happened unto you" (1 Peter 4:12, KJV).

Peter writes to the church that is scattered at that time because of persecution to encourage them in the various things they were going through. Reading it in the King James Version, you would think Peter was about to release a word of instant miracle because he starts with the word "beloved." Yet the word he gives to those who are loved dearly by God is "Do not be surprised by what you may go through."

Peter feels it imperative that his readers understand they need to expect suffering. The worst thing that can happen to us in any life scenario is to be caught off guard. Being caught off guard by an event can alter your life forever.

I have seen people get hit by an unexpected problem and totally lose who they were because they were unprepared for the level of adversity that struck their lives. Peter is prepping the church by saying, "Do not be surprised."

The teaching of Peter and the earlier example from Job are so much different than the brand of Christianity we have delivered to people today from our pulpits. Very little is said about going through. Very little is said about dealing with extended trouble. And that is why, in my opinion, when people go through anything of any length, they quit. They give up. They abandon the house of God. They return to a former vice of life. It is all because they did not expect to go through anything. They did not anticipate any trouble. They thought their lives would be the fairy tale; happily-ever-after story promised to them if they came to Jesus.

Yet again, the apostle Peter is shouting from his platform about *fiery trials*. We need to wake up and realize that life will be full of challenges. It will be necessary for us to have a strategy to get through these things.

So as we get started on this journey to get through what we are going through, I wanted to share that everything I am writing about was birthed as I was meditating on Isaiah 43:2. As I read it, I thought to myself, *It is so interesting that God speaks to His people about going through and not just instant deliverance in this verse.*

Look at it closely with me:

> When thou passest through the waters, I will be with thee; and through the rivers, they shall not overflow thee: when thou walkest through the fire, thou shalt not be burned; neither shall the flame kindle upon thee. (Isaiah 43:2, KJV)

Here we can clearly see: God has already anticipated for the children of Israel that some days ahead would be troublesome. If you are familiar with the background of Isaiah, you know that when you get to chapter 43, Isaiah is transitioning from severely rebuking Israel to providing a much needed word of comfort and hope. In this chapter, God speaks to His people as their *Creator*. God has a special and unique claim upon them because He is their Creator, yet according to what we see recorded here, knowing Him as Creator will not exempt them from calamities and afflictions. And apparently, their troubles were going to be extreme. Why do I say extreme? Because He uses extreme terms "when you pass through the waters and rivers" and "when you walk through the fire." Extreme. Sounds extreme to me.

Water and fire are proverbial phrases for extreme perils and dangers. God said to them, "*When* you go through them," not *if* but "*when* you go through them." God was saying, "Hey people, I dearly love you guys very much, but just know there will be some extreme things that are going to happen. Don't say I didn't warn you."

So here is what I believe: getting through what we are going through is enhanced by understanding a few truths that are imperative.

- First thing, everybody goes through. The words written to open this chapter are true: "Into each life some rain must fall." No one is exempt. No one gets a pass. Sure, there are people who seemingly have less hassle, but everyone gets hassled.

- Secondly, it does not mean God does not love us because we are going through. The preachers have promised us so much prosperity and blessings that sometimes we feel like God does not love us because we are going through a trial. It is a lie. God loves us dearly. Remember, He called the children of Israel "beloved" before He broke the news to them about going through. We are extremely loved by God.

- Thirdly, it does not mean we are not Christians if we are going through. This mind-set is again the result of the "only blessings" messages. Somehow, we have fashioned a theology that Christians do not go through. This teaching misrepresents scripture. The Bible is a balanced book. It has all the special scriptures we underline, commit to memory, and quote on a regular basis about blessings, but it also has the neglected admirations which speak of "suffering persecution" and "enduring hardness." If you are going through, it does not, in any way, indicate that you are not a believer.

- Next, it does not mean we have committed some cardinal sin if we are going through. This is one of my pet peeves here. I grew up in church, and there was a time that if you were going through anything, it had to be because you had sinned. You could not have a common cold without someone pointing a finger at you to accuse you of doing something wrong.

It reminds me of the story in the Bible of the guy born blind in John chapter 9. The question the disciples asked Jesus was the prevailing mentality of the time in which it was asked, "Master, who did sin: this man or his parents that he was born blind?" Jesus had to set the matter straight, and he did so quickly with this response, "Neither hath this man sinned nor his parents."

The point is don't allow people to put condemnation on you because you are going through.

Another classic example is Job. Job had three investigators, I mean, friends, who came to visit him as he was processing through his trouble. They attempted to get Job to confess his wrongdoing, but Job had nothing for them. Each of his friends took a turn at rebuking Job because there had to be some sin somewhere.

The rebuke of Zophar seems to have been the most stern and direct of the three. He says, "If only you would prepare your heart and lift up your hands to him in prayer! Get rid of your sins and leave all iniquity behind you" (Job 11:13–14, NLT).

Job's response was "I know as much as you do. You are no better than I am. As for me, I would speak directly to the Almighty. I want to argue my case with God himself" (Job 13:2–3, NLT). Job was not having it. He was not going to allow condemnation to settle in his spirit despite the accusatory tone of his buds.

- Additionally, it does not mean we are not as favored as someone else who is not going through. Favor is one of the biggest catch words in the body of Christ these days. People are walking around declaring they are "blessed and highly favored." I love it because I, too, am blessed and highly favored. Yet the reality is blessed and highly favored people go through too. And if you go through something that someone else is not going through, it does not mean that you are not as favored as they are.

God does not have respect of persons. By the way, you may be going through it because you can handle it, whereas if they went through it, they may fold up like a wet paper bag. I'm just saying.

- Finally, it does not mean that something strange is happening because we are going through. Again, rain falls into everyone's life. We are not being picked out to be picked on; we are all picked on. It is not strange that you have to deal with so much. Remember, we are children of God, and just as Job was chosen to endure and win, we should believe nothing less.

The Importance of Prayer

S lavery was a major sin in the history of America. It has been estimated by Patrick Manning, president of the World History Network, Inc. that about 12 million slaves entered the transatlantic slave trade between the sixteenth and the nineteenth century. Of those 12 million, 10.5 arrived in the Americas.

Initially, efforts to proselytize these transplanted Africans were futile in the United States. Only a few of them were willing to convert to a gospel message that was so far removed from anything they had ever been taught. Even the great John Wesley, who founded Methodism, went to Georgia to attempt to evangelize both native Americans and African slaves. When his missionary efforts proved ineffective, he got on a boat and headed back to England.

It was around the time of the Great Awakening that slaves began to accept, in significant numbers, the gospel. The first recorded black congregation was organized on the plantation of William Byrd near Mecklenburg, Virginia, in 1758.

The gospel message taught slaves to believe in God, to pray, to hope, and, against the wishes of many slave owners, the gospel inspired within the slaves a desire to be free. Yet here they were going through slavery.

God did not instantly deliver the slaves as soon as they became followers of Christ. From the time of the first black congregation to the end of slavery was 107 years. Do not miss that 107 years.

During the 107 years, one of the most important things that the slaves learned to do was to pray. The slaves would even have their own secret prayer meetings outside of the normal Sunday morning worship services.

A former slave by the name of Wash Wilson recalled from his own experience what happened at these covert gatherings.

> When [us] go round singin' 'Steal Away to Jesus,' dat mean dere gwine be a 'ligious meetin' dat night. De masters…didn't like dem 'ligious meetin's so us natcherly slips off at night, down in de bottoms or somewhere. Sometimes us sing and pray all night.

Notice the activity of these people in bondage—singing and praying all night. How did this help? Why did they do it? Something within them (I believe the Holy Spirit) caused them to realize that if they were going to get through what they were going through, they needed to worship, and they needed to pray.

Of these two disciplines, I want to zero in on the latter, the discipline of prayer and its importance whenever we have an unfavorable circumstance happening in our lives.

Of course, many books have been written and sermons given on the subject of prayer. This chapter will, no doubt, probably remind you of things you already know, especially if you are a seasoned veteran in the body of Christ. Yet these reminders will be imperative for you to get through what you are going through.

As a pastor of a church for more than twenty-five years, I am always amazed at the many people who come to my office for counseling concerning some issue that has been plaguing their life, and yet, they have not uttered one prayer in the direction of heaven about the situation. I listen as intently as possible and then hit them with the question, "Have you prayed about this?"

They respond with the dumbfounded deer in the headlights look and then guiltily answer *no*. Really? No prayer! How do we expect to make it through any adversity if we neglect the importance of prayer?

I recently read an article called, "Science Proves the Healing Power of Prayer" on newsmax.com. In the article, Duke University's Harold G. Koenig MD tells Newsmax Health about an exhaustive analysis of more than 1,500 reputable medical studies about prayer. Koenig says, "Studies have shown prayer can prevent people from getting sick, and when they do get sick, prayer can help them get better faster." Well, who does not want to get better faster? I certainly do.

Koenig added, "The benefits of devout religious practice, particularly involvement in a faith community and religious commitment, help people cope better. In general, they cope with stress better, they experience greater well-being because they have more hope, they're more optimistic, they experience less depression, less anxiety, and they commit suicide less often. They have stronger immune systems, lower blood pressure, and probably better cardiovascular functioning." Dr. Koenig just preached!

The words I cannot shake in Dr. Koenig's statement is that prayer helps us cope. That is what we all are searching for when we are going through, a way to cope with it without losing our minds or gunning somebody down in the street from the overwhelming stress of the situation.

Prayer helps us to get through our situations in the godliest way possible.

When Paul and Silas were locked in jail—the way they coped with the misery of the situation was the same way the slaves did. (I guess I should say the way the slaves coped was the same way Paul and Silas did. They did come first.) Paul and Silas, at midnight, sang songs and prayed.

At no point does the scripture say that they prayed for a miracle release. We are not told they prayed for an earthquake to come and rattle their cell and set them free. Maybe they did. But I believe their prayer was more just to cope with the situation. To get them through the night, if you will.

The Bible has within it the story of a woman named Hannah. She was going through barrenness. Along with barrenness came embarrassment, a sense of rejection, and a feeling of failure. That is because women without children were looked at as less than a woman during the time she was dealing with her circumstance.

Hannah was a prime candidate for depression and medication. She should have been popping some sort of Percocet or antidepressant, but the girl knew what to do. In the midst of the chaos she was going through, she felt one of the best ways to get through was to pray. So we find her in the book of 1 Samuel chapter 1.

> And she was in bitterness of soul, and prayed unto the LORD, and wept sore. And she vowed a vow, and said, O LORD of hosts, if thou wilt indeed look on the affliction of thine handmaid, and remember me, and not forget thine handmaid, but wilt give unto thine handmaid a man child, then I will give him unto the LORD all the days of his life, and there shall no razor come upon his head. And it came to pass, as she continued praying before the LORD, that Eli marked her mouth. (1 Samuel 1:10–12, KJV)

I love verse 12. It says of Hannah, "she continued praying." She teaches us a very valuable lesson: do not stop praying.

Praying is appropriate at all times and in all circumstances. Praying is the key to sustaining a right attitude and proper response to whatever life may deal us. Prayer is a willingness to trust the faithfulness of God to His promises and to His people. Hannah is an example of someone who was going through, and her prayerfulness was effective. She prayed, and God answered her prayers!

What I want you to learn to do when you are going through is to be prayerful. Again, do not stop praying. Never stop praying. Luke 18:1 (KJV) says, "Men ought to always pray and never faint."

Why are we so committed to the discipline of prayer? Well, I am glad you asked. The commitment to prayer arises from an awareness that our need can only be met by God.

I have heard many believers saying we should only pray for something once and then leave it to God. I believe when you have not received your answer, you do not just stop. The more you pray, the more you are expressing to God, "Lord, I am aware this need can only be met by You."

Prayerfulness then demonstrates a continual trust in God. It emphasizes we are totally reliant on God and will not give up on His ability to come through. When I say, "Come through," He is going to come through with the answer; He is going come through with the miracle or He is going to come through with strength to help us make it another day and peace not to lose our minds.

Prayerfulness needs to be maintained, especially in difficult circumstances. Satan's job is to get us to give up. Prayer helps us to win the battle over our minds. Prayer places our thoughts in the heavenly realm rather than trying to persevere using our own thinking. So what I am trying to say about prayerfulness is prayerfulness keeps us conscious of God's ability to intervene.

For this reason, child of God, pray. Regardless of what you are going through, pray. Pray because we are commanded to do so. Pray because it builds our relationship with God. The closer we sense we are to Him, the less effect the problem can afflict upon us.

Pray because it changes us. They say prayer changes things, but I believe prayer changes us as well. Here's the point. If what we are going through does not instantly change because we prayed, prayer still is important. Prayer helps us to cope with our situation without compromising our trust in God's ability to respond to our need when He is ready to respond. We can handle the wait better.

Pray because prayer is warfare against the enemy. The devil hates a praying believer. When he has thrown everything he can think of at you to aggravate you, you, in turn, aggravate him greatly by turning to God, not to curse Him but to bless Him by connecting with Him in prayer.

Finally, pray because prayer is the pathway through. If you are going to make it through what you are going through, prayer is the pathway.

The Importance of Patience

Good things come to those who wait. I'm sure you have heard that before, huh? Does it make you as angry as it makes me? It is not what I want to hear when I am going through.

Notwithstanding, we have to realize that another strategy to implore whenever it is necessary to get through what we are going through is patience. As a matter of fact, the scriptures tell us that we should mimic the examples of previous believers who used patience to get to their promise. The scripture that purports this doctrine clearly is Hebrews 6:12 (KJV), "That ye be not slothful, but followers of them who through faith and *patience* inherit the promises" (italics in the scripture was added by me).

Whenever the Bible encourages us to follow an example, it does so for a reason. The reason is clearly because whatever means are used by the example will be the same means we will need to implore to be as successful as they were.

The writer of Hebrews focus in this verse is on those who through faith and *patience* inherited promises. He does not have in mind those who received anything instantly because he would have not used the word patience. He is highlighting believers who had to wait on God. He is putting the spotlight on those who had to go through what they had to go through before inheriting their promise.

In the next chapter, I'm going to use this same verse to talk about faith; but in this chapter, I want to just dive in on the importance of patience.

Whether we realize it or not, most people do not travel on the quick path to their blessing, their healing, or their miracle. Most people take the long winding road. Most people go through something to get to something. I hope you realize this. Sure, the ones we hand the microphone to are those who had an extraordinary miracle happen as soon as they opened their mouths and asked for it; but the pews are full of believers who have had to wait—people who had to be patient.

Look at what Paul tells the church at Rome, concerning how to best deal with trouble. He writes to them in order to share a needed exhortation. "Rejoice in our confident hope. Be patient in trouble, and keep on praying" (Romans 12:12, NLT).

Why Are We Told to Be Patient?

The reality is that God works on His time and feels no pressure to work on our time. Contrary to our belief, God does not just come when we want Him to come. He comes at His appointed time and not ours.

God has the liberty to miss our deadline, to completely ignore our timeline, and to express absolutely no obligation to our schedule. We may not like it, yet we better understand it. This type of illumination demands that we exercise patience.

What Is Patience?

Patience is the capacity to accept or tolerate delay, trouble, or suffering without getting angry or upset. In another book I read, it said, "Patience is waiting without complaint." It is not enough to say you have patience while your behavior exhibits anger. Sorry, that is not patience. Patience is not just what you do, patience is manifested in how you do it. If you are grumbling and complaining, you are not operating in patience. By definition, patience is not getting upset or griping about the process during the process.

Why do we need patience?

Patience is required because it is our tendency to see things only from our own point of view. We cannot see what God is doing.

When we cannot see what God is doing, we become aggravated and impatient. It is the aggravation that causes us to lash out in anger or become upset.

After the children of Israel are delivered from the Egyptians in the Old Testament and are advancing toward the promised land, they begin to run out of patience with the circumstances they are dealing with in the wilderness. They consistently murmur and complain about their meals, their water, their conditions—just about anything they could think of bellyaching about. At one point in the narrative, God runs out of patience with them.

In a conversation with Moses, He tells Moses He is about to disown them and make another nation through Moses (Numbers 14:12). Moses has to pray and ask God not to destroy the people. Whew, and thank God, God listens.

The issue is that it can be very detrimental to our own well-being to be impatient. Not using patience can cause us to make poor decisions that affect our future in a negative way. I cannot tell you how many times people have expressed to me their remorse for not waiting on God. When you don't wait on God, you end up with something you wish would disappear. When you do not wait on God for your spouse, you may end up with the one you wish you never had. When you do not wait on God for His timing in everything, you put your own happiness and even life at peril.

There is trouble in Abraham's house in the Old Testament. Sarah, his wife, is in an uproar. She is perturbed. She is angry. Her anger stems from seeing her son Isaac being mocked by her stepson Ishmael. Yet, if we properly investigate the story, we come to realize the reason Isaac is troubled by Ishmael is because of an impatient recommendation by Sarah. God had promised a son through Abraham and Sarah. This son had yet to be produced after an extensive amount of time had past. Sarah had lost her ability to wait and recommended to her husband to have a sexual encounter with her handmaiden. Their amour produced the boy Ishmael.

Ishmael is what we get when we are not patient. And now Ishmael, the thing manufactured in impatience, is getting on Sarah's nerves.

As we are getting through what we are going through, patience then is for our benefit. Using patience means we can be persistent and stay in something for the long run and allow God to perform His promise. Patience keeps us from cutting corners or doing things in an unethical way; instead, we patiently let things work out, we do what needs to be done, and make things happen.

How do we develop patience?

That's the question that everyone is searching for the answer. Whenever I hear a message about patience, I realize I am operating from a deficit. So how do we develop patience?

The writer of the book of Hebrews was rather straightforward with the Jewish Christians when he wrote what was recorded in Hebrews 10:36 (KJV), "For ye have need of patience, that, after ye have done the will of God, ye might receive the promise." Pretty rude, huh? He did not cut them any slack in his analysis. He assessed the situation and came out with a diagnosis that did not need to be interpreted. "You have need of patience"! Bam!

Okay. So again, how do we get patience? How is it developed? According to scriptures we can come to several truths concerning patience. First, patience is produced by the Holy Spirit. It is a part of the fruit of the Spirit that Paul writes about in Galatians 5:22 (NLT). "But the Holy Spirit produces this kind of fruit in our lives: love, joy, peace, patience, kindness, goodness, faithfulness." When the Spirit comes into our lives, He comes with patience. In order to get this patience operational, we must yield to the Holy Spirit. When we refuse to yield to the Spirit, we quench His operational status. When He, the Spirit, is dormant, we can only operate by our flesh. The flesh is impatient.

Another way patience can be granted is through prayer. We can pray for patience. We can have others pray for our patience. The apostle Paul prayed for the church at Colossae in Colossians 1:11 (NLT). He says, "We also pray that you will be strengthened with all his glorious power so you will have all the endurance and patience you need. May you be filled with joy." Isn't that the prayer we all hope God would answer for each of us? All the patience we need, do it, Lord!

Next, patience can be gained through tribulation. Seriously, I am not signing up to get patience this way, but we cannot ignore the fact the Bible teaches this lesson. Again, it is from the pen of the apostle Paul. This time, he is writing to those in Rome. He writes, "And not only so, but we glory in tribulations also: knowing that tribulation worketh patience" (Romans 5:3, KJV).

Did you see it? Tribulation works patience. Nothing teaches like experience. When we experience tough times and then witness God performing a miracle on our behalf, it instills in us the ability to trust and wait on God the next time we are confronted with a similar challenge.

So as we are getting through what we are going through, it is imperative to remember why we should employ patience in our situation. It is patience that gives us the ability to not give up. Patience aggravates the devil. He wants us to move on our own whims. He wants us to bail on God's plan as soon as we encounter any extensive trouble. However, when we respond in patience, when we just put things in God's hands and ride out whatever storm is happening, there is not much the devil can do to defeat us.

Another important aspect of patience is that it allows things to manifest in God's perfect timing. Timing is everything. There is a time and season for all things. Whenever God decides to get you through what you are going through, you can be guaranteed His timing will be impeccable. God does all things well and at the perfect time.

Finally, patience produces maturity. James, the brother of Jesus, writes, "But let patience have her perfect work, that ye may be perfect and entire, wanting nothing" (James 1:4, KJV). This scripture shows us that patience has a job to do. Sometimes people say they have to do something about their situation, but in reality, patience is doing something. There are times where we are going to have to let patience do her perfect work.

The work of patience is to mature us into well-developed believers. Patience solidifies our trust in God as being the source for all blessings we receive. Patience in trouble is not a popular response, but it is one we must employ.

The Importance of Faith

I n the last chapter, we dealt with patience. This chapter, we will deal with patience's cousin—faith.

Faith refers to "trust in God." It involves trusting in the future promises of God and waiting for their fulfillment. Faith is to surrender final control of one's life over to God. To lack faith is to give in to one's desire for control.

Hebrews 11 has always been known as the Hall of Faith for believers. It is where we clearly see the importance of faith in action by those who walked this earth long before we got here. It shows how they used faith, kept the faith, and were motivated by faith to get through what they were going through.

I almost feel like there is no need for me to write much in this chapter. Hebrews 11 is an amazing composition, showcasing people who displayed faith in God. I can just put the words of Hebrews 11 right here on these pages, and it would suffice to explain the importance of faith in getting through what we are going through.

I challenge any believer to grab your Bible and encounter the words. It will bless your life. Some highlights are:

- "It was by faith that Abraham obeyed when God called him to leave home and go to another land that God would give him as his inheritance. He went without knowing where he was going" (Hebrews 11:8, KJV).
- "It was by faith that Jacob, when he was old and dying, blessed each of Joseph's sons and bowed in worship as he leaned on his staff" (Hebrews 11:21, KJV).

- "It was by faith that the people of Israel went right through the Red Sea as though they were on dry ground. But when the Egyptians tried to follow, they were all drowned" (Hebrews 11:29, KJV).
- "All these people earned a good reputation because of their faith, yet none of them received all that God had promised" (Hebrews 11:39, KJV).

Let's talk about just these four scriptures and what we see, remembering from our last chapter that we are to be "followers of them who through faith and patience inherit the promises" (Hebrews 6:12, KJV).

The first guy is Abraham. Abraham is told to leave his home and go somewhere, not even knowing where somewhere was.

Allow me to emphasize how stressful and overwhelming that had to be for Abraham. Please do not underestimate what he had to be going through to obey this word from God. Yet he exercised faith to make an unfamiliar journey.

So although the journey you are on is unfamiliar to you, have faith. God knows where you are going, and He intends to show you how to get there.

Next up, Jacob. Jacob is dying but still is able to exercise faith. He is going through his own dilemma but decides to bless others through his faith. That is interesting.

Even while we are going through what we are going through, we can exercise faith by blessing others. While we are blessing others, it allows us to be able to push through whatever season we may be facing. You may be going through the toughest episode of your life, but you are still a valuable asset to people in your circle. Use your faith to bless them. There will be amazing results experienced by those whom you bless.

Hebrews 11:29 shares an account about the children of Israel. The children of Israel went through the Red Sea by faith. Can you imagine what it really took to go through a sea? Can you imagine how daunting it had to be to step in this divided sea and trust that God was not going to allow it to close in on them?

That is a word for you! You are going through and seeing the most difficult situations before you, and now you have to trust that God will not allow your world to close in on you.

To take your first step, it is going to take faith. To make it through it, it is going to take faith. To get to the other side, it is going to take faith.

Then finally, Hebrews 11:39 talks about all the other people who did not get everything God had promised them, but it was not because of a lack of faith. Sometimes faith may not get you to your blessing, yet it may get you through life to be rewarded with a better place.

Many times, God's people were required to display faith when there was no visible finish line and no feeling of relief from the problems they were encountering, yet they kept their faith. Any time you deal with biblical faith, you have to be honest about things. Many people, in the Bible, believed in what God spoke to them, even though some did not see things come to pass in their lifetime. I am sure they were disappointed or confused at times not seeing things come as they had thought; yet they had faith in their God. And God commended them for their faith.

When you are going through, you should never abandon your faith in God. Remember the quote of the three Hebrew boys of the Old Testament—Shadrach, Meshach, and Abednego? These three were getting ready to be tossed in a fiery furnace for refusing to worship anyone but Jehovah. Just before they were catapulted into the fire, they ensured their captors that God was well able to deliver them, even in the fire. However, if He did not rescue them, they still would not in any way have a change of mind. They were still resolved to go into the fire and face death while maintaining their allegiance and faith to the one true God.

Some may ask, therefore, so then why have faith if it does not guarantee deliverance from my present dire circumstance? If my faith will not just make it happen, why have it?

First, faith pleases God! Hebrews 11, verse 6 shines the brightest light possible on this truth. It reads, "Without faith, it's impossible to please God because anyone who comes to Him must believe that he exists and that He rewards those who earnestly seek Him."

In the gospels, we see a story of a man who had God-pleasing faith. In Matthew 8, Jesus runs into a centurion, a high-ranking soldier in Capernaum. This centurion has a servant at home who is sick of a disease called palsy. The palsy is a medical term which refers to various types of paralysis,[2] often accompanied by weakness and the loss of feeling and uncontrolled body movements such as shaking.

When the centurion tells Jesus about the servant, Jesus tells him, "I will come and heal him."

The centurion was like "No, don't come to my house. I am not worthy of that." But he said, "Speak the word only!"

When the Savior heard that, He was like "Boy, what did you say?"

Jesus said, "I haven't seen faith like this in all Israel." He is thoroughly pleased with the faith of the centurion.

In this case, the centurion's servant is healed in the same hour he amazes Jesus with his faith. Again, do not miss it; faith pleases God.

There is so much more to learn about why we should have faith, and one of the best passages to learn it from is by enjoying some more of the narrative in Hebrews 11 about these faith heroes. Hebrews 11:32–40 (KJV) drops this insight on us:

> How much more do I need to say? It would take too long to recount the stories of the faith of Gideon, Barak, Samson, Jephthah, David, Samuel, and all the prophets. By faith these people overthrew kingdoms, ruled with justice, and received what God had promised them. They shut the mouths of lions, quenched the flames of fire, and escaped death by the edge of the sword. Their weakness was turned to strength. They became strong in battle and put whole armies to flight. Women received their loved ones back again from death. But others were tortured, refusing to turn from God in order to be set free.

[2.] https://en.m.wikipedia.org/wiki/Paralysis.

They placed their hope in a better life after the resurrection. Some were jeered at, and their backs were cut open with whips. Others were chained in prisons. Some died by stoning, some were sawed in half, and others were killed with the sword. Some went about wearing skins of sheep and goats, destitute and oppressed and mistreated. They were too good for this world, wandering over deserts and mountains, hiding in caves and holes in the ground. All these people earned a good reputation because of their faith, yet none of them received all that God had promised. For God had something better in mind for us, so that they would not reach perfection without us.

Let's glean three things from these verses although there is so much more there. Through these three things, we come to understand the importance of faith a little more. The first thing that jumps out at us is this: sometimes God blesses those who trust Him with spectacular results.

Gideon and the crew mentioned in verses 32 through 35 do some remarkable things through their faith. They are victorious against nations, nature, and death. Their faith turns their weakness into strength. God works spectacular things through faith.

Even today, yes, today, we implore faith because we still believe spectacular results are available to whoever can believe. God is still a miracle worker. Do not be fooled by all the naysayers. Do not even be fooled by the title of this book. God can give you a miracle that changes everything, and He can do it today! I believe. Do you?

However, and this is the reason I share this, if for whatever reason, beyond our limited understanding, the spectacular does not immediately occur, we recognize, point two, sometimes God blesses those who trust Him with the grace to endure horrible trials without wavering (11:35–38).

The history of God's people is replete with examples of people who lost limbs and even lives but without compromising their faith in the Lord. The fact they are able to endure the wicked and calculated attacks against them is a testament to their faith.

Today we implore this same faith because we know enduring trials is just as much a spectacular result as an instantaneous miracle!

Finally, God will bless all who trust Him with eternal rewards (11:39–40).

In another chapter in this book, we will deal with having an eternal view concerning what we are going through as being important to get through what we are going through.

It is interesting that none of the heroes of faith received everything God promised. This is really speaking about the Messianic era of the New Covenant which we now live in. The heroes of faith never saw the Messiah they waited to see. Yet with eternity in mind, both the living and the dead will be transformed together to live with the Lord. As one commentary puts it: the past and present generations are bound together in God's purpose.

The ultimate glorification of the saints is only possible through Jesus Christ, and consequently, the heroes of Hebrews and each believer today will reap the same eternal rewards for what they have had to endure for the Lord while on this earth.

The Importance of Joy

Georg William Cooke was born in Yorkshire, England, in 1884 and became a minister associated with a group called the Gospel Crusaders which was connected with the Methodist Church. He ran the Delmarva Camp, a Methodist camp that held Gospel meetings and revivals. He was later minister of Methodist churches in Buffalo and Rochester, New York.

Cooke was a writer of Gospel hymns. The one I remember singing as a child growing up in church was copywritten by Cooke in 1926. The words were

> I have the joy, joy, joy, joy
> Down in my heart
> Down in my heart
> Down in my heart
> I have the joy, joy, joy, joy
> Down in my heart
> Down in my heart to stay

This joy Cooke wrote about is a joy that is embedded in his heart forever. It is not a temporary joy. It is not a passing joy. It is a permanent joy. It is down in his heart to stay. It is joy that will not leave. It is a joy that will not vacate his life just because his life dynamics change. It is a joy that remains and refuses to be uprooted by anything.

Joy is extremely important to all believers and vital to assist us in getting through what we are going through.

In 1407, a man by the name of William Thorpe was imprisoned for his beliefs as, what will become known more than a century later, a Protestant Christian. He wrote about his experience of dealing with his time behind bars. It is interesting in his writing to note how important joy, rejoicing and praise were to allow him to properly deal with his fate. Thorpe writes,

> And so then I was led forth and brought into a foul unhonest prison where I came never before. But thanked be God when all men were gone forth then from me, and had barred fast the prison door after them…[I] busied me to think on God and to thank him [for] his goodness.
>
> And I was then greatly comforted in all my wits, not only because I was then delivered for a time from the sight, from the hearing, from the presence, from the scorning, and from the menacing of mine enemies; but much more I rejoiced in the Lord, because that through his grace he kept me so, both among the flattering and among the menacing of mine adversaries.

James, the bishop of the church at Jerusalem, has a word from God he needs to distribute to the Jewish believers to encourage them to endure and live bold Christian lives. They were being persecuted for their faith and dealing with the most severe hardships. In his letter to them, he drops this word on them, "My brethren, count it all joy when ye fall into divers temptations" (James 1:2, KJV).

In the New Living Translation, the same verse says, "Dear brothers and sisters, when troubles of any kind come your way, consider it an opportunity for great joy."

The exhortation here is to bear trials with a cheerful mind. James tells the church to count it all joy when different temptations come because he knows these things are not working against them; they are actually working for them.

That is one of the truths that alludes us as we go through. Things are not actually working toward our detriment but toward our benefit.

Someone shared with me, after I had made a statement like this in one of my messages, that they had too much going on for it to be true that things were actually going to be beneficial for them. And, if this was how they were feeling, how could they operate in joy? The truth of the matter is we have to choose not to allow ourselves to be overwhelmed by the complexity nor the intensity of what we may go through. We take charge of what we are dealing with by operating in joy.

Joy is birthed from understanding that the intensity of our trouble does not change the fact that God is in control, redeeming all things for our benefit. The scripture remains true; all things work together for our good, and this is why we can count things as joy.

The apostle Paul gives his insight on this subject in Romans 5:3 (NLT). "We can rejoice, too, when we run into problems and trials, for we know that they help us develop endurance." I love the words, "we can rejoice."

Again, this is a choice. This is something within our ability to do. We can rejoice. Rejoicing is based on what you know. Joy is based on what you know. According to Paul, what we know is that endurance is being developed when we run into problems and trials.

Then there are Peter's words found in 1 Peter 4:12–13 (NLT). They speak volumes. He writes,

> Dear friends, don't be surprised at the fiery trials you are going through, as if something strange were happening to you. Instead, be very glad— for these trials make you partners with Christ in his suffering, so that you will have the wonderful joy of seeing his glory when it is revealed to all the world.

The exhortation here is to be very glad; to have joy rather than to frustrate yourself by trying to figure out how trials have come into your life. Nothing strange is happening, but something supernatural is. These trials we go through validate our partnership with Jesus Christ, and we are guaranteed to be witnesses of His glory.

What does it mean to "count it all joy" as James puts it? It means, in short, that there is nothing in afflictions which ought to disturb our joy. And thus, he not only commands us to bear adversities calmly and with an even mind but shows that there is a reason why the faithful should rejoice when pressed down by them.

Joy is defined as a positive human condition that can be either feeling or action. The joy scripture commands are mainly joy in action. This joy is engaged in regardless of how the person feels. For instance, the Bible implores men to rejoice in the wife of their youth without any reference to what the wife may be like now (Proverbs 5:18). Jesus implores His disciples to rejoice when they are persecuted, reviled, and slandered (Matthew 5:11, 12).

The word *rejoice* in the scriptures is a command to "have joy."

Joy is not like happiness which is based upon happenings or whether things are going well or not. No, joy remains even amidst the suffering. Joy is not happiness.

Happiness comes from happenings. Happiness is predicated on something good happening to us or for us. As soon as the happening is over or has grown old, then we are no longer happy concerning the matter. Joy remains joy even when the circumstances are not joyful.

The prophet Habakkuk is a great model of a man who makes the decision to have joy based upon hope even if present situations are turbulent. Habakkuk is in the place of praying for God to bring revival to Israel and to avenge her of her enemies. Habakkuk is so beaming with hope that he will not allow the possibility of trouble to disintegrate his hope. He brazenly declares that although the fig trees do not blossom, and there are no grapes on the vine and the olive oil fails and the fields are empty and the flocks die and the cattle barns are empty, these things will have no effect upon him. For Habakkuk has made a choice, and we read of his choice in Habakkuk 3:18 (KJV), "Yet I will rejoice in the LORD, I will joy in the God of my salvation." Habakkuk chooses to rejoice.

How can we have the joy of Habakkuk? How can we have the joy of George Cooke? How can we have the joy of William Thorpe? How can we have the joy James asks of us? How can we have the joy Peter and Paul asks of us? How can we have the joy Jesus asks of us?

Joy, my friends, is a by-product of life with God, and it is found in the Holy Spirit of God. Having the Spirit of God is such a phenomenal benefit for us as believers. As a part of the fruit of the Spirit we find, yep, you guessed it, joy. Paul told us this, "But the fruit of the Spirit is love, joy, peace, longsuffering, gentleness, goodness, faith, meekness, temperance: against such there is no law" (Galatians 5:22–23, KJV).

Joy is also found in the presence of the Lord. Psalm 16:11 (KJV) provides this insight. "Thou wilt shew me the path of life: in thy presence is fulness of joy; at thy right hand there are pleasures for evermore."

So as we are thinking about the importance of joy as we are going through, I believe we have to study a proverb. This proverb is important because it explains why being in the right spirit or right state of mind when life attacks is so significant. Let Proverbs 18:14 (KJV) settle in your heart, mind, soul, and spirit. "The spirit of a man will sustain his infirmity; but a wounded spirit who can bear?"

Notice a wounded spirit; a melancholy, broken spirit; a sad, crushed spirit is not something that serves us well when we are trying to handle an adverse situation. It takes being in the right spirit to have victory when we face our toughest days.

Joy puts us in the right spirit and does not allow the broken spirit to rule our thoughts or behavior. Additionally, the Bible adds, "A merry heart doeth good like a medicine" (Proverbs 17:22, KJV). We need medicine when we are managing pain. I have my go-to pills when I feel any physical discomfort. I am sure you do too. It is joy that can lead us to a place of healing if we can grasp its importance as we are going through.

Finally, where there is joy, there will also be on display a believer who refuses to quit. Joy is a sustaining power. A joy response is important and essential to get us through trials. Things could have gone much differently for Paul and Silas if they had not been so joyful in that Philippian jail. In the story in Acts 16, when they sang songs at midnight while they were in those stocks, it allowed their spirits to remain strong. Joy helped them to get through their midnight experience.

The Importance of Endurance

Eusebius was a Christian historian. He lived in the late 200s into the early 300s. He was able to chronicle a lot of what the early, developing church had to face. In Ecclesiastical History book 8 chapter 3, he shares some observations concerning how the Christians were going through during one of the times of persecution the church faced.

> Vast numbers of the prelates of the church endured with a noble resolution the most appalling trials and exhibited instances of illustrious conflicts for the faith…Here was one who was scourged with rods, there another tormented with the rack and excruciating scrapings, in which some at the time endured the most terrible death; others were passed through other torments in the struggle…there another, lying upon the ground, was dragged a long distance by the feet.

Isn't it amazing what believers in antiquity are willing to endure for their relationship with Jesus Christ? Isn't it equally amazing, or more so, what we call "going through" in the twenty-first century?

The early church would probably laugh hysterically at us for what we now put in the category of going through. This is not to say we do not legitimately face our own modern day complexities as believers, and like the church of old, we must be willing to endure.

Endurance is not a big subject from the pulpits these days. Yet, in the history of the church, endurance was key to the survival of the Christian movement. Those who named the name of Christ understand that bearing the name would make them candidates for torture, humiliation, suffering, and even death. We, too, even to this day, must be ready to endure the things we are purposed to go through for the sake of Jesus Christ.

Let's grab a scripture you may know. It comes from 2 Timothy 2:3 (KJV). "Thou therefore endure hardness, as a good soldier of Jesus Christ."

Here is the apostle Paul in this verse offering an important piece of encouragement to one of his sons in the Gospel, Timothy.

Commentary writers have written that when Paul wrote these words, he had in mind that some believers had deserted him because he was in prison. His imprisonment was a cause for concern because if Paul, a spiritual leader, was in prison, no doubt, those associated with him would soon be locked up too. Paul did not want Timothy to follow the examples of those, who for fear of imprisonment, had abandoned him. Instead, Paul was asking Timothy to follow his example. Since Paul was enduring hardness, he expected his spiritual son to follow suit.

Paul was a prototype of suffering. He had been through trial after trial as a Christian. Yet he was unbroken. He wrote this:

> Three times I was beaten with rods. Once I was stoned. Three times I was shipwrecked. Once I spent a whole night and a day adrift at sea. I have traveled on many long journeys. I have faced danger from rivers and from robbers. I have faced danger from my own people, the Jews, as well as from the Gentiles. I have faced danger in the cities, in the deserts, and on the seas. And I have faced danger from men who claim to be believers but are not. I have worked hard and long, enduring many sleepless nights. I have been hungry and thirsty and have often gone without food. I

have shivered in the cold, without enough cloth-
ing to keep me warm. (2 Corinthians 11:25–27,
NLT)

I am sure that with all this drama happening in his life, Paul
has to consider at one time or another whether or not he should
just drop out on God; yet he endures. Now he is telling Timothy
to endure because Paul does not believe that what he experiences is
unique to him, neither does he believe that endurance is unique for
him. He understands that every Christian must expect some measure
of ill-treatment from life.

Why? Why must we suffer? Why must we go through? After all,
we are children of God. We are more than conquerors. We are the
head and not the tail. Why are we ill-treated with all that working
for us?

There is a devil. Hopefully, I did not shock you with my last
sentence. There seems to be a lack of awareness in some circles of
Christianity, concerning the realness of the devil. This fallen angel
who was kicked out of heaven is the archenemy of God; and thereby,
an archenemy of God's greatest creation—man. This means he is
trying to break us all. He is trying to get us to give up and tap out.

He knows where and how to attack each of us. He has a play-
book on each of us with the intention to dissolve our resolve. His goal
is to steal our push, passion, and ultimately, our purpose. Knowing
this about the adversary we all have, Paul exhorts Timothy and us,
too, to endure.

Endurance is essential to get us through what we are going
through. We have to have endurance.

Let's give definition to this word endurance. Endurance is the
act, quality, or power of withstanding hardship or stress. For believers, endurance is continuing in their Christian commitment in the
face of difficulty. Endurance is also the ability to persevere in a task
or calling.

Paul uses the soldier as the example of how a Christian is to
endure. Why the soldier? Well, the main reason Paul uses a soldier is
because this is war! We are in a warfare against Satan and his fallen

angel friends. He hates everyone who serves Christ; and therefore, we have to be ready to be warriors. This is war!

I spent twelve years in the US Army as a journalist. My job afforded me the opportunity to see all aspects of training the army used to prepare its warfighters for endurance. I will never forget being assigned to do a story on a survival, evasion, escape, and resistance course being taught to a group of soldiers. I was taken aback by the intensity of training these troops faced as they were pushed to the limits of exhaustion while facing nearly impossible scenarios they needed to endure. They were being exposed to these things because in war, anything can happen.

War is brutal. If a soldier falls into the hands of the enemy, he needs to expect the harshest conditions and treatment. A soldier needs to have an endurance mind-set.

Well, when it comes to the army of the Lord, too many people are more *quit*-ready than *endurance*-ready. We used to sing songs like, I'm a soldier in the Army of the Lord. It seems like today we have deactivated our units and retreated into hiding.

We need to be soldiers. We need to endure hardness. We need to be ready to dig in and not quit. It is time to call the warriors back to active duty. The point Paul is making is that soldiers endure because they understand warfare. Their mindset is locked on endurance.

There are particular things soldiers do to enhance an endurance mind-set. Paul elaborates on these in 2 Timothy 2:4 (KJV), "No man that warreth entangleth himself with the affairs of this life; that he may please him who hath chosen him to be a soldier."

First, endurance is enhanced by eliminating distractions. If we are going to endure, we cannot allow unnecessary things to distract us.

Again, with my twelve years of military experience, I remember quickly understanding how the duties of military service had to take precedence over civilian affairs. In the old Army, they used to say to guys who had to do something for or with their wives during duty hours, "If the Army had wanted you to have a wife, they would have issued you one." The message in this was when you are in a fight, you cannot be distracted by outside concerns because if you do, you may not survive the fight.

Paul is saying this so we will be ready to renounce everything which hinders the real purpose of the soldier of Christ. There is nothing wrong with other things except when these things entangle us and cause us to quit.

Secondly, Paul tells Timothy endurance is enhanced by focus. He wants Timothy to focus on pleasing the Father who chose him. God's choice is undeserved. There is nothing so great about us to be His soldier. His choice is simply motivated by His grace. Since He has been so gracious to us, it makes perfect sense that we live our lives in a way that pleases Him. When we are driven by gratitude and the desire to please God, endurance is a natural result.

Athletes who play a team sport are, many times, familiar with this drive. Many times, you will hear them talk about how they play for their coaches or they go all out for their coaches. There is a sense of gratitude for them being chosen for the team and for the investment the coaches make into their development.

Therefore, no matter how tough the practice or the game, they find an inner fortitude to endure it in order for the coach or coaches to be pleased. How much more should we be focused on pleasing Jesus Christ? When we have a single-minded devotion to Jesus Christ, there is nothing that can defeat us or sway us.

It reminds me of the story of Bishop Polycarp of Smyrna who was facing death for his devotion to Christ. Polycarp is given an opportunity to recant his beliefs but famously responds, "Eighty and six years I have served Him, and He has done me no wrong."

This type of devotion to Christ will get you through anything. You may be saying, "Didn't Polycarp die for his devotion?" Well, yes, he did.

Sometimes Christians die. It is an honor to die for Christ going through whatever you have to go through without compromising love or commitment to Him.

To get to this level of endurance, we must strive to become deeply rooted in the word. Where there is no word, there will be no endurance.

Jesus explains this in his parable about the sower going out to sow. He draws particular attention to the rocky soil that some seeds fall on.

> The seed on the rocky soil represents those who hear the message and immediately receive it with joy. But since they don't have deep roots, they don't last long. They fall away as soon as they have problems or are persecuted for believing God's word. (Matthew 13:20–21, NLT)

The message of living for Christ is a message to be received with joy. It is a message of hope. It is a message that has the propensity to change our lives. However, if the message does not get rooted deep within us, the message is in jeopardy of not sticking. The New Living Translation says the message "will not last long"; and here is the issue: when problems or persecution come, if the message is not rooted, we will fall away because the word has been eradicated by the worry associated with the problem.

The Word of God has to be deeply rooted in us if we are going to survive valley experiences and disappointing episodes during life. It is by recalling the Word of God and rehearsing the Word of God that we are able to endure.

Many prisoners of war used the Word of God to enable them to bear up under the cruelty of imprisonment.

One such prisoner was Howard Rutledge. Rutledge was shot down over Vietnam and served as a POW for seven years. Later he wrote a book about his ordeal and gave a powerful testimony as to the importance of Scripture. He endured brutal treatment, sometimes shackled in excruciating positions and left for days in his own waste. Rats, the size of cats, crawled around his cell, but he was quoted in an article written by Jan White in the Andalusia Star News dated November 12, 2011.

> "Everyone knew the Lord's Prayer and the Twenty-third Psalm," but the camp's favorite verse, the one that prisoners recalled first and quoted most often, was John 3:16, "For God so loved the world, that He gave…"
>
> He described how much time he spent trying to remember what he heard growing up in Sunday School and was amazed at what he did recall. Looking back, he realized the importance of memorizing verses from the Bible.
>
> "I never dreamed that I would spend almost seven years (five in solitary confinement) in a prison in North Vietnam or that thinking about one memorized verse could make the whole day bearable," he relates.
>
> One portion of a verse he did remember was "Thy word have I hid in my heart" (Psalm 119:11). He regretted not hiding more of God's Word in his heart.
>
> The former POW states, "Scripture and hymns might be boring to some, but it was the way we conquered our enemy and overcame the power of death around us."

They quoted memorized scriptures to make the day bearable is what Mr. Rutledge remembers. This is a lesson from which we all can benefit. Whatever we need to endure becomes more bearable when God's word is introduced to the circumstance.

The Word of God has a way of soothing doubts and calming fears. The Word of God has a way of putting us into a victorious state of mind. That is why it is so important to get it deeply rooted in us.

Another thing that enhances endurance is preparation. Remember, the survival training I observed, this was preparatory work. This was preparing men and women to survive. We should all be training to endure, knowing trouble is going to come to us all in one capacity or another.

I live with my family in North Carolina. Living in North Carolina places us in the way of many hurricanes. We are fortunate to have meteorologists who bombard our news programs with predictions of these monster storms. Wisely, whenever one is headed for a direct hit, we head for the Walmart. We buy batteries. We buy water. We buy milk. We buy bread. We buy a generator. We do all these things to prepare to endure the hurricane. We are preparing not just for the hurricane but also the aftermath of the hurricane when the power may be out, and we are potentially stuck in our homes for several days.

Knowing trouble comes to us all, we should prepare ourselves to endure it. So many people become demobilized because when things hit, they say, "I did not see that coming." Well, beloved, get ready; things are coming.

The apostle Paul explains to the Colossians what he is praying about concerning them. He writes in Colossians 1:11 (NLT), "We also pray that you will be strengthened with all his glorious power so you will have all the endurance and patience you need."

This is the same verse I used in the chapter on the importance of patience. Along with all the patience they need, Paul's request to God is that these people receive all God's glorious power so they would have all the endurance they need as well. He is not just talking about having endurance for the present, he wants them to be equipped to endure whatever may befall them in the future. He wants them to have all the endurance they will ever need.

As a part of the package of our salvation, we receive the Holy Spirit. The Holy Spirit has fruit. A part of that fruit is endurance. Endurance comes from the Spirit and is the mark of a true Christian. Here is Galatians 5:22 (KJV) again, "But the fruit of the Spirit is love, joy, peace, longsuffering, gentleness, goodness, faith."

The word we should pay attention to in this narrative, for the sake of our discussion, is long-suffering. It is another word for endurance.

Long-suffering denotes long and patient endurance. God supplies us with endurance when we receive His Spirit. It is an expected outcome of having the Spirit of God that we will be able to endure. Did you hear that? You will be able to endure. Endurance verifies the presence of God's Spirit in our lives.

When we think of long-suffering, we think of God. God is long-suffering toward us. He puts up with our mess, our blatant ignoring of His existence, our continual disobedience of His principles, and our constant disregard for a close relationship with Him; and He stills loves us and calls us to Himself.

His ability to endure me is one of the most amazing acts of God I have witnessed in my life! His endurance is amazing. Now with His Spirit residing in us, we are given the same ability to endure.

I said all that to say, it is the Holy Spirit of God, in addition to the Word of God, that prepares us to endure. The Holy Spirit not only supplies us with the ability to endure but also warns us, as the meteorologists do, when impending storms may be on the way. We should be filled with the Holy Spirit every day of our lives.

The Gospel singer Kirk Franklin released a song called "I Smile" on his twelfth album entitled, "Hello Fear." In the song, he speaks of how some days have no sunshine and feel like cold nights. The lyrics report that there are days that lack the love and joy that were promised and as a result hurt sets in. At one point of the song, it says (please catch it), "I'll be honest with you. I almost gave up but a power that I can't explain, fell from heaven like a shower!" This power Mr. Franklin is speaking of is the power of the Holy Spirit. He is the one who helps us to endure and to smile through it all when we would have given up without His help.

So what is the importance of endurance? Well, earlier in this chapter, I said that this is war! Endurance is meant to get us through every battle we face. Endurance gets us to the end; endurance gets us through what we are going through.

Jesus addresses the power of endurance with His disciples. He knows their faith and fortitude would be tested. He tells them, "And ye shall be hated of all men for my name's sake: but he that endureth to the end shall be saved" (Matthew 10:22, KJV).

Haters come. We cannot allow the hate to cause us to lose focus on what God has promised. We have to endure people. We have to endure problems. We have to endure life.

One of the great places in scripture where we can regain our focus when we begin to become weary is found in the book of James. James, the brother of our Lord, knows the saints of his time are dealing with some difficult times. He ensures them that "Blessed is the man that endureth temptation: for when he is tried, he shall receive the crown of life, which the Lord hath promised to them that love him" (James 1:12, KJV).

Endurance reaps eternal rewards. We will discuss this further near the end of this book.

The Importance of Courage

Fear is one of the most powerful forces on the earth. Fear stops dreams. Fear disables potential. Fear brings success to a halt. Fear robs of destiny and purpose. Fear is a powerful force.

The Bible is full of admonitions to *fear not* for a purpose. Everyone battles fear. If we are going to experience success in every aspect of our lives, we are going to have to know how to overcome fear. If we are going to get through what we are going through, then fear must be trampled upon and eradicated out of our mindsets.

When I finished high school, I went into the army at seventeen years old because my family could not afford to send me to college, and I was not sure I wanted to go anyway. After four years of serving, I decided to take advantage of an opportunity to pursue a degree in communications since it was what I was doing in the military.

College was going great until fear made an unwanted appearance and brought my academic pursuits to a screeching halt. What was the problem? Speech class. You read that right, speech class. I was too afraid to stand up in front of other students and give a speech. I dropped the class. There was no way to get the communications degree without the class, so I also dropped out of college. All because of fear.

In 1 Corinthians 16:13 (NLT), these words are written, "Be on guard. Stand firm in the faith. Be courageous. Be strong." Paul writes this verse in the latter part of his letter to the church of Corinth. He is giving them some final declarations, some final words to remember. His words to them are concise yet comprehensive. They are simplistic yet profound. They are easy words to remember and could be presented as a daily to do list for the church.

There are four significant things he admonishes them to do:

1. Be on guard.
2. Stand firm in the faith.
3. Be courageous.
4. Be strong.

We would be better off as Christians if we put much emphasis on the instructions he lists here. All these instructions beg to be written about, but I am going to stay on task in this chapter and only deal with one.

Paul says be courageous. And here is the thing about this strong encouragement: Paul would never tell them to do something that was not within their ability. When Paul says be courageous, he has every expectation that it will happen.

Perhaps we should put a definition to the word *courage*.

What is courage? One dictionary defines courage as "the state or quality of mind or spirit that enables one to face danger, or fear, with confidence, and resolution." Courage is bravery.

Courage, for the believer, is not predicated on physical strength or physical ability. For the believer, courage is the ability to always rely upon the supernatural power of God to strengthen him to overcome, or to get through what he is going through. Therefore, courage comes from the supplier of courage, not from our own strength. God is the supplier of courage.

Whenever we are going through, it is our tendency to be afraid of an outcome, and this fear is only overcome by courage. When we do not know how things will pan out when we are going through a difficult time or facing a momentous challenge, we will need to be courageous. Courage counteracts fear.

Way back in the 1980s and '90s, there was this ferocious fighter by the name of "Iron" Mike Tyson. He was purported to be the most feared heavyweight boxer of all time. This guy destroyed his opponents. Usually he was done with his challenger within two rounds. I actually went to watch him fight on closed circuit TV (Google it) against Michael Spinks in 1988.

In my opinion, Spinks was already defeated before the fight begun. As the ring announcer introduced the fighters, it looked like I saw complete utter fear in the eyes of Spinks. Ninety-one seconds after the bell sounded to begin the fight, it was over. Spinks was out for the count, and Tyson had won again.

On February 11, 1990, Tyson walked into the ring with a 37–0 record, with thirty-three knockouts, to face what was surely to be another KO victim, a former *basketball player*, James "Buster" Douglas. This fight was different however. About three weeks before the fight was to take place, Douglas's mother died. When Douglas entered the ring in Tokyo, Japan, he was not just fighting for himself anymore, he was fighting for his mom.

Douglas stood toe to toe with Mike Tyson for eight rounds. In that eighth round, a familiar scene happened. Tyson caught Douglas with a right uppercut that knocked him on his butt. Surely, this fight had taken a little longer, but it was about to produce the same outcome. Tyson had done it again. However, this fight was different. Unexpectedly, Buster Douglas got up!

Sometimes when you use your courage to get in a fight, it does not mean you are not going to be hit or even knocked down, but then you are going to have to be courageous enough to get back up and fight on. Douglas was courageous enough to get up and start fighting again.

You can do that too. You may have been knocked down with one of life's most vicious uppercuts, and you are considering just lying on the canvas and allowing life to count you out. Get up! Be courageous.

Two rounds after being knocked down by that powerful uppercut, Douglas unleashed one of his own, snapping Tyson's head skyward. Douglas followed it up with a quick combination and, to everyone's surprise, knocked Tyson to the mat. It was the first time, in his professional career, that Tyson had been knocked down, and he would not get up. Douglas had prevailed because he was able to show courage.

In the Bible, one of my favorite characters is Joshua. Joshua has the daunting task of replacing Moses as the leader of God's chosen people, Israel. Moses has done the improbable. He leads the children of Israel out of slavery to the Egyptians and defeats the army of the Pharaoh. Moses's only failure, so to speak, is that he does not get the nation to the promised land. This endeavor is passed on to Joshua.

Joshua is shaking in his boots at just the very thought of replacing his mentor Moses. When the burden of responsibility is squarely laid on his shoulders, he is probably wishing that God would choose someone else. God is not going to do that. Instead of choosing someone else, God gives Joshua a commandment. God says, "This is my command—be strong and courageous! Do not be afraid or discouraged. For the Lord your God is with you wherever you go" (Joshua 1:9, NLT).

Think about this: this is a command, an authoritative order. In an earlier chapter, I told you I was in the military. One of the things we were taught early in the process was not to question orders. It was our duty to execute orders, not question them. Here we have the commander of all commanders handing out orders to Joshua, and his orders are "be strong" and "courageous!"

How was Joshua just going to be strong, just like that? Is there some magic, hidden button that we do not know about that can be switched on and off at will?

God commands Joshua to be strong and then supplies the rationale behind this order. "For the Lord your God is with you wherever you go." God is with us.

I am going to deal with an entire chapter on the guaranteed presence of God and how important it is to get us through what we are going through, so keep reading.

The thing to accept now is God has every expectation we will begin walking in courage rather than fear based on the simple truth that He is with us.

At this point, we should address the importance of courage in getting through what you are going through. You can never win a fight that you do not show up to participate in. You will never win a contest by not coming on the field. This is call forfeiting. The thing about forfeiting is it takes away any chance of a victory.

Fear robs of the chance to overcome. Fear robs of the chance to get through what we are going through. You are going to have to show up.

Life can be so rocky at times. We can feel like just lying in the bed, pulling the covers over our heads, and hopefully whatever challenges we are facing will magically disappear. Unfortunately, this is not how it works. We cannot just cower in the bed. We have to grab a hold of courage and show up.

It takes courage to battle cancer, to battle for the marriage, to battle for joy; and this courage is within you, and God is commanding you to use it by, first of all, just showing up.

The amazing thing about having the courage to show up and take on what has been trying to defeat you is God will reward your courage with His power. Courage allows us to continually tap into the power of God, and the more He supplies, the more courage we get.

Therefore, do not fear what is going on. Do not fear what you are attempting to get through. Fear is from your enemy, the devil. God has not given you a spirit of fear (1 Timothy 1:7). God has given you power—power to believe, power to stand, power to endure, power to win. Only be strong and courageous. We have to realize we have it in us to be courageous and to keep going!

The Importance of Doing the Right Things

"Pressure bursts pipes." I cannot tell you how many times I have heard this in my lifetime. The general meaning is when we are under tremendous stress in life, it can cause us to break and do something out of character or, in the case of the believer, something out of the will of God.

Going through is pressure, especially when it prolongs. The longer we go through, the more aggravated we can become.

We all have heard of the person who just could not take what they are dealing with in life anymore and decides to take their own life. This is pressure bursting the pipe. What they were going through could have been a divorce, or the loss of a job, or a sickness, or a legal problem—whatever it was, it broke them. We should never underestimate the propensity for pressure in any trying situation. If not careful, any of us could do something out of character. We can lash out at others. We can steal. We can become bitter and distant. It is a list that can go on and on.

With that in mind, this chapter's focus is the importance of doing the right things. Here is where we will begin: Galatians 6:7–9 (NLT). It is written there,

> Don't be misled—you cannot mock the justice of God. You will always harvest what you plant. Those who live only to satisfy their own sinful nature will harvest decay and death from that

sinful nature. But those who live to please the
Spirit will harvest everlasting life from the Spirit.
So let's not get tired of doing what is good. At
just the right time we will reap a harvest of blessing if we don't give up.

Since we all go through one thing or another, one thing after
another, I believe most of us would agree with this statement: when
we are going through, it is easy to become tired of doing the right
thing. Amen? And when we get tired, we are tempted to become discouraged, to slack off, even to give up. It is called burnout.

We can become tired of living right, tired of acting right, tired
of giving, tired of serving, tired of doing, tired of doing what is good.
Becoming tired of doing the right things can be recognized by statements birthed from utter frustration. Like if your spouse has committed adultery, and you start saying, "I'll get him or her back by doing
the same thing," this statement is in complete conflict with your faithful character and is only being uttered because you are tired of the
stress that has come with the knowledge of your spouse's infidelity.

Paul recognizes our probability for weariness. In Galatians 6,
Paul is giving the church at Galatia some of his final instructions
on being a Christian, things like relating to others and growing as a
Christian. Paul masterfully begins a discussion of sowing and reaping.

Believe it or not, it is not a money conversation either, rather
it is for us to understand the importance of how we react to life as it
comes.

The lesson is this: whatever we sow, that is what we are going to
get in return. This is so important to understand when you are going
through a difficult season.

Going through is not the time to sow bad seed. It is not the time
to let weariness cause you to act out of character. It is not the time to
allow bad confessions or statements to spill out of your mouth. As Job is
going through his myriad of problems, he is approached by his wife. She
is observing the plight her husband is in, and she seems to have come
to the conclusion that God is somehow at fault. Her analysis causes her
to pressure Job to say something. She brazenly advises her husband to

"curse God." Thankfully for Job, he still has enough strength to emphatically refuse to comply to her potentially damaging request.

Job's response was "Woman, you sound foolish." He follows that statement with a quite profound way to look at life when you are getting through anything. Job remembers the good days. He remembers the blessed times. He remembers what God has done.

With this in mind, he asks, "Shall we accept good from God and not any trouble"? Job realizes that trouble does not change the fact that God loves him dearly and would continue to love him dearly.

Sadly, most of us realize God's love for us, yet unfortunately, we do grow weary of doing good. We do grow weary of still doing the right things. Why do we grow weary anyway? We grow weary because no results are coming about. No change is happening. Nothing new or different is starting to develop. We aren't seeing anything. So since we aren't seeing anything, we stop doing the good we know we should be doing. We stop serving in ministry. We stop going to church. We stop being concerned for others. We act out and do not care what God thinks because we are tired of holding on until our change comes. Is it worth it, we ask?

Yes, yes, it is worth it. Pay attention to 1 Corinthians 15:58 (KJV), "Therefore, my beloved brethren, be ye steadfast, unmovable, always abounding in the work of the Lord, forasmuch as ye know that your labour is not in vain in the Lord."

Sowing good seed is never a worthless endeavor. Doing good when we are getting through what we are going through is the sowing of good seed. This type of labor is not in vain. It reaps a good harvest on the other side of what we go through.

Earlier I mentioned Job refusing to comply to the request of his wife to curse God. His strength results in a good harvest being produced once he is able to get to a place of deliverance from the onslaught of the devil.

If you have been in church any length of time, you have heard the term "double for your trouble" most likely. This term is birthed out of the end of Job's story where God gives him twice as much as he lost.

What we need to remember though is the end of the story is many times predetermined before the end. The end is determined by what happens in the middle. What seed has been sowed? What words have been uttered? What faith has been executed? We have to sow the right seeds in order to get the right harvest.

Everything we do has consequences. The incentive for doing good should be the fact we know there is a due season coming. With this in mind, it should regulate all our activities. Farmers do what they do with the due season in mind.

The due season is the season known to the farmer as harvest time. Harvest time is when reaping takes place. I do not know about you, but I want to reap what is known as "the believer's reward." What is that? It is when we do what we are supposed to do, and then we get what we are supposed to get. The kingdom principle of sowing and reaping is always in full effect. Watch what you do.

Rev. Dr. Martin Luther King Jr. is one of my heroes. He was a principled man. He was a leader whom God raised up at the appropriate time to deal with the blatant sin of racism that plagued our country. Dr. King was committed to doing the right things as he led the cause of civil rights.

Dr. King was a proponent of nonviolence. The oppressors were not proponents of the same. Blacks were lynched, bitten by dogs, sprayed by water hoses, beaten by police officers, imprisoned, spat on, cursed at, and treated inhumanely. Dr. King's philosophy of nonviolence, of doing what he felt to be the right thing, was severely tested. There were many people who felt the need to abandon the nonviolent concept and began going tit for tat with those who were fighting against the movement. King resisted the counter ideals with as much consternation as he could display.

In Dr. King's first book *The Stride Toward Freedom*, he outlined his six principles of nonviolence. These principles are so interesting that I will share them with you now.

1. Principle 1—Nonviolence is a way of life for courageous people.
    *   It is active nonviolent resistance to evil.
    *   It is aggressive spiritually, mentally, and emotionally.

2. Principle 2—Nonviolence seeks to win friendship and understanding.
    *   The end result of nonviolence is redemption and reconciliation.
    *   The purpose of nonviolence is the creation of the Beloved Community.

3. Principle 3—Nonviolence seeks to defeat injustice not people.
    *   Nonviolence recognizes that evildoers are also victims and are not evil people.
    *   The nonviolent resister seeks to defeat evil not people.

4. Principle 4—Nonviolence holds that suffering can educate and transform.
    *   Nonviolence accepts suffering without retaliation.
    *   Unearned suffering is redemptive and has tremendous educational and transforming possibilities.

5. Principle 5—Nonviolence chooses love instead of hate.
    *   Nonviolence resists violence of the spirit as well as the body.
    *   Nonviolent love is spontaneous, unmotivated, unselfish and creative.

6. Principle 6—Nonviolence believes that the universe is on the side of justice.
    *   The nonviolent resister has deep faith that justice will eventually win.
    *   Nonviolence believes that God is a God of justice.

These principles were keeping the movement on track. These principles were instrumental in providing the strides of progress that our country has made. Sure, we still have a long way to go, but doing the right thing when another option was available is the lesson we learn from Dr. King's principles.

The Importance of the Guaranteed Presence of God

> He (God) is the most magnanimous of captains.
> There never was his like among the choicest of
> princes. He is always to be found in the thickest
> part of the battle. When the wind blows cold he
> always takes the bleak side of the hill. The heavi-
> est end of the cross lies ever on his shoulders.
> (Charles Haddon Spurgeon)

These are the words of one of the most famous preachers of all times—Charles Haddon Spurgeon. It is said that Spurgeon is history's most widely read preacher except for the Biblical ones.

During his lifetime, Spurgeon is estimated to have preached to 10 million people. He died in January 1892. The excerpt above is from the last sermon he ever preached. He was only fifty-seven years old when he died. His prolific preaching did not exempt him from going through in life.

Spurgeon's cross to bear was sickness. He went through debilitating gout and recurring depression. Yet we find him extolling the virtues of God to always be found in the heat of the battles of life and always to be there to help shoulder the load of any cross. Spurgeon could not find a time where God was an absent Father. He was always there.

In a previous chapter, I wrote about how God had handed the assignment of leading Israel from Moses to Joshua. Joshua is confronted with filling the shoes of the greatest leader known to the Jews up until that time. This is an overwhelming responsibility. A part of God's marching orders to Joshua are to be courageous. So just like that. Joshua had to tighten up his belt and just do what God had commanded him to do.

The reason why he is to be courageous is because God tells Joshua, "I'm with you wherever you go." I call this God's guaranteed presence. It is the guaranteed presence of God that assures us that we can make it through whatever we have to deal with in life.

Let's revisit one of the base scriptures this book is based upon in order to begin to allow the beauty of this truth to resonate in our spirits.

> When thou passest through the waters, I will be with thee; and through the rivers, they shall not overflow thee: when thou walkest through the fire, thou shalt not be burned; neither shall the flame kindle upon thee. (Isaiah 43:2, KJV)

It is the A clause of this verse that I want to draw your attention to in this chapter. Hopefully you see it. God says to Israel, "When thou passest through the waters, *I will be with thee.*" These five key words from God are the ones I want to resound in your spirit: "I will be with you." This is God Himself making a promise that He will not break.

God has never and will never be in the promise breaking business. This is God Himself saying of Himself that He will be there in the waters with Israel. That is why I am boldly and unapologetically using the word *guaranteed*.

To say that something is guaranteed means that without a doubt or without question, it is going to happen. The dictionary definition of *guarantee* is something that assures a particular outcome or condition.

I want you to absolutely know that as you are getting through what you are going through, God guarantees you that His presence will be there. Just as He told Israel, when you go through the waters, I will be with you. He is telling each and every one of us, when we go through, He will be with us.

Here is a little background on chapter 43 of Isaiah. God is in the process of renewing His commitment to Israel concerning protection and deliverance. If you know the history of the book and the people of Israel, you know there was a need for God to severely rebuke them for their sins, and He does so sternly. Yet as is so often the case, the rebuke is followed by comfort and consolation. Israel is assured that God has not cast them off! Their sin was not great enough to cause God to change His mind about them.

As far as their future, God was able to peer into their future and tell them there will be some afflictions ahead, but when passing through them or getting through them, He was going to be right there with them. They were being guaranteed His divine presence during troubles of any kind. He was going to be a personal escort for the entire nation of Israel.

It reminds me of what Paul writes in Romans 8 about how nothing can separate us from God's love for us, and then he supplies an exhaustive list of things: tribulation or distress or persecution or famine or nakedness or peril or sword—none of these things we go through has the capability of separating us from God's love. Wherever God's love is, so is His presence.

I do not care what our trouble may be, God's presence in our lives doesn't change. Just know He says, "I will be with you." Whatever God says, He does.

When God speaks to Joshua about His guaranteed presence, Joshua is probably saying to himself, "How am I going to handle this task? It's too big for me. What do I do? Where do I go?"

God interrupts his mental anguish and, in so many words, tells him to chill, based on the fact that "I am with you wherever you go."

Joshua could not make a move where he would be able to shake the presence of God, neither could Joshua make a mistake and God allow him to find his way by himself. Catch this: God said, "I am with you wherever you go," not just wherever I send you.

So whatever we may go through, be it by the direction of God, the attack of Satan or whether we have mismanaged our lives, still God is with us wherever we go.

In the New Testament, the disciples received a similar word on the guaranteed presence. In the very last verse of Matthew 28, which is verse 20, this is the Word of the Lord to them: "Teach these new disciples to obey all the commands I have given you. And be sure of this: I am with you always, even to the end of the age" (NLT).

I love how the New Living Translation uses the words "be sure of this!" This is a guaranteed word. God's promise is, "I am with you always even to the end of the age." There is an additional revelation here about the guaranteed presence of God that we should make sure we understand in this verse.

In the scriptures we have digested about His presence so far— His presence has dealt with location. In other words, wherever you are located, I will be there.

In Matthew 28, this is not a word about location, being with you wherever you go, but duration. "I am with you until it is over. I will be with you until the end of the age."

God is not just with us until His patience runs out with us dealing with whatever we are going through, God wants us to know He is there for the duration. God has made a decision. His decision is to personally engage Himself and dwell among the children of God in all places and at all times.

Knowing God will be with us should bring both comfort and confidence to us children. Comfort and confidence are keys to getting through what we are going through. It is like when the child is afraid of perceived "monsters under the bed," and daddy comes into the room and gets up under the covers, the child immediately experiences a comfort and confidence that eventually leads to a good night's rest.

Thinking of that reminds me of one of my favorite verses of all time in the Bible. It is one I live by, especially when faced with going through any adversity. It is Psalms 23:4 (KJV), "Yea, though I walk through the valley of the shadow of death, I will fear no evil: for thou art with me; thy rod and thy staff they comfort me."

David in Psalm 23 preaches a prolific message in such a short passage. First, he comes to grips with the fact that sometimes you have to go through a valley. We cannot escape the valley. We cannot bypass the valley. We have to go through the valley. David's valley is named the valley of the shadow of death. Our valley can be called a valley of sickness, a valley of depression, a valley of loss, a valley of poverty, a valley of marital strife, the list can go on and on. Yet in his valley, David has come to an impressive and educated decision to "fear no evil." I am impressed and awed by the decision because, again, his valley is called "the shadow of death!" If his valley was made into a movie, I am not going to see it at the local IMAX theater. It sounds absolutely frightening to me. The *Valley of the Shadow of Death* starring Freddy Krueger! No, thanks.

I call David's decision educated because it is based on what he knows. What does he know? He knows the Lord is with him. Some may wonder, what is so important about that? Here is the lesson. Since God is with David, he can and he will make it through the valley experience. No matter where the valley may take him (location) or how long it may take to get through it (duration), David is assured of the guaranteed presence of God. This presence supplies David with comfort and confidence.

There are three things I believe God's guaranteed presence secures for every believer.

1. His presence secures our protection. God will protect us as we go through whatever we may be facing.

    In the story of Job, the devil wants unlimited access to Job in order to afflict him in any way he desires, however God put restraints on his activity in order to protect Job. You may be saying, "All that Job went through, and you are saying God protected him?" I absolutely am. God knows what Job can bear and only allows afflictions at His discretion. The thing we have to remember when we are getting through what we are going through is that everything that happens in our lives is filtered through the hands of God.

2.   The guaranteed presence of God secures peace for us. There was a song sang by the Mississippi Mass Choir back in the day. The song was entitled "Having You There." The lyrics that I remember so well are words that were sung to God. The choir sang,

> We have come to praise and magnify the Lord.
> For all that He has done and for
> the victories we have won.
> In the good times and in the bad times, in
> the happy times and in the sad times;
> having You there, made the difference,
> just having You there.

Just having God there calms our fears and gives us peace. Again, it is like daddy coming to get in the bed when the perceived monsters may jump out at any given moment, or so the child believes. Dad's presence brings peace and allows a restful night.

3.   The guaranteed presence of God secures victory for the believer.

Now victory is a subjective discussion. God chooses to give victory to the saints in various ways, and if we are not careful, we can miss victory when it occurs.

Most of us would say that victory means I come out of what I am in and get blessed with "double for my trouble." However, God may determine victory to be that you survived the process. That's it. Period. Or victory may be that you held on to your relationship with God in spite of what was done to you.

Again, I am reminded of the church father, Bishop Polycarp, who was taken to be burned at the stake on February 23, AD 155. Surprisingly enough, one of the accusations against Polycarp was that he was an atheist because he did not believe in the Roman gods. He was an adamant defender of the Judeo Christian teachings of there being only one God. As he approached the fire, he was given a way out of what he was going through. All he had to do was denounce Christ. He would not. He did not. This was his victory! He was able to maintain victory by holding on to his relationship with God.

This is why in the next chapter, I am going to share about the importance of having an eternal view. We are, many times, so focused on the here and now that we overlook the real purpose for our reconciliation to God. It is about eternity!

The Importance of Having an Eternal View

Light after darkness, gain after loss;
Strength after weakness, crown after cross;
Sweet after bitter, hope after fears;
Home after wandering, praise after tears;
Sheaves after sowing, sun after rain;
Sight after mystery, peace after pain;
Joy after sorrow, calm after blast;
Rest after weariness, sweet rest at last;
Near after distant, gleam after gloom;
Love after loneliness, life after tomb;
After long agony, rapture of bliss;
Right was the pathway, leading to this. (Unknown)

The words above were written by some unknown source who was captivated by the soon coming glory of eternity and heaven. The emphasis being how wonderful heaven will be in comparison to the many challenges we face while living on this globe.

In the New Testament, we find Jesus speaking a lot about the eternal. As Jesus was beginning His journey toward death, His disciples were becoming increasingly aware that His departure was necessary to the plan of God. Nonetheless, the necessity of His departure was no less hurtful. Jesus had to give them hope. He had to get them to focus on something beyond how they were feeling at that moment.

So here is what He says to them: "Don't let your hearts be troubled. Trust in God, and trust also in me. There is more than enough room in my Father's home. If this were not so, would I have told you that I am going to prepare a place for you? When everything is ready, I will come and get you, so that you will always be with me where I am." This, of course, are words found in the beginning of John 14 (NLT).

Jesus was shifting their focus from what was presently happening in time to what was going to happen in eternity. Although they were going to have to go through seeing their Master die and eventually be taken away from them, knowing eternity awaits them, where they will forever be with Jesus, was meant to soften the blow.

In our day, it is becoming increasingly more difficult to get people to realize this world is not more important than eternity. What we go through down here will easily be eclipsed by the joy of what is next—heaven. Jesus lived life with an eternal perspective in mind, and I believe we should as well. After all, He is our example.

If you did a study on the Sermon on the Mount, you would probably be amazed at how many times Jesus steers the conversation toward the eternal. Those who are pure in heart, He says, will see God. Those who are persecuted for righteousness sake are told, theirs is the kingdom of heaven. Those who are reviled and spoken of falsely are told to rejoice because great is the reward of heaven. Those who teach the commandments of God will be great in heaven. These were just some of His exhortations recorded in Matthew 5. Eternity and heaven are a big deal for Jesus. Eternity and heaven should be a big deal for us as well.

One of the best examples of Jesus's focus on the eternal is seen in the book of Hebrews. There, the author records these words "Looking unto Jesus the author and finisher of our faith; who for the joy that was set before him endured the cross, despising the shame, and is set down at the right hand of the throne of God" (Hebrews 12:2, KJV).

What does the scripture tell us about Jesus?

The first lesson that bears repeating is Jesus is our pattern. We are told to observe Him. Look unto Jesus. The pattern of life has been cut by the maker of life. If we are going to learn how to endure anything, there can be no greater example than Jesus who knows the brutality of death on a cross was going to be His lot in life. He had to go through the cross, just like many of us will have to go through something.

The second clear lesson is Jesus is our supplier. He is the author and finisher of our faith. He supplies faith to us. We have a faith that He has birthed in us by Him. Not only did He birth the faith, but He also preserves the faith and finishes the work of faith in us. In other words, the faith matures in us. The faith becomes a faith that is not soon shaken or bothered by life's adversities. It becomes a faith that can handle what life may dish out.

The third lesson we learn from this is where Jesus chose to put His focus. There was a joy set before Him. That joy was eternity. That joy was heaven. That joy was to go back to be with His Father. Everything He did, He did with going home in mind.

So because of the joy He knew awaited Him in eternity and with this eternal mind-set, He went through what He had to go through. He endured the cross. Sure, the cross brought Him shame and agony because it was the most deplorable criminal death in Rome at that time. Yet He went through it based on knowing the reward. When He went to take His seat by the right hand of the Father, the pain of enduring the cross paled in comparison to the reward of being reunited with the Father.

Our reward for serving God through Christ here on this earth and dealing with the struggles and strongholds of life, and remaining faithful is heaven. Please do not get me wrong. I am enamored by the benefits of our salvation, like most people are, blessings upon blessings; but the real reward is heaven. Heaven is what we are living for and waiting to enter into.

The apostle Paul is a man thoroughly acquainted with going through. His résumé does not quite read as elaborately as the modern day preacher fluff that we see on personal web pages. Remember, Paul's résumé speaks of being three times beaten with rods, once being stoned and dragged out of a city as dead, three times being shipwrecked, once bitten by a snake, and once spending a whole day adrift at sea. Paul also faces dangers from rivers and robbers, dangers from Jews and Gentiles, and dangers in cities and deserts. He also self-reported, many sleepless nights and many days of being hungry and thirsty. Yet, when Paul thinks about what is to come, these words found themselves being put to paper by the apostle: "For I reckon that the sufferings of this present time are not worthy to be compared with the glory which shall be revealed in us" (Romans 8:18, KJV). Paul reckons that what is to come is much more glorious than what is happening now.

Again, the conversation Jesus has with his disciples in John 14 starts with "Do not be troubled by what you are going through." Then He immediately diverts their attention from the present to the future.

He follows with, "I'm going to prepare a place for you." These words are intentional. Our mind-sets must be heavenly, especially while we encounter stress and strain from life events; heaven will need to be on our minds. Here is another scripture that clearly reveals this.

> Since you have been raised to new life with Christ, set your sights on the realities of heaven, where Christ sits in the place of honor at God's right hand. Think about the things of heaven, not the things of earth. (Colossians 3:1–2, NLT)

I love reading what John Gilmore wrote in *Probing Heaven: Key Questions on the Hereafter*.

> Suffering both increases our desire for heaven and prepares us for it. John Bradford (1510-1555), less than five months before his fiery departure from life for preaching the gospel in violent times, wrote to a friend of the glories of heaven he anticipated:
>
> I am assured that though I want here, I have riches there; though I hunger here, I shall have fullness there; though I faint here, I shall be

refreshed there; and though I be accounted here as a dead man, I shall there live in perpetual glory.

That is the city promised to the captives whom Christ shall make free; that is the kingdom assured to them whom Christ shall crown; there is the light that shall never go out; there is the health that shall never be impaired; there is the glory that shall never be defaced; there is the life that shall taste no death; and there is the portion that passes all the world's preferment. There is the world that shall never wax worse; there is every want supplied freely without money; there is not danger, but happiness, and honour, and singing, and praise and thanksgiving unto the heavenly Jehovah, "to him that sits on the throne," "to the lamb" that here was led to the slaughter, that now "reigns" with whom I "shall reign" after I have run this comfortless race through this miserable earthly vale.

Undoubtedly, we go through. We have major catastrophic events that sometimes rock our world. We have to go through. But please understand we get through it better with a heavenly mind-set.

Here is one more passage that again teaches us the importance of adjusting our mind-sets to the eternal. Once again, the apostle Paul is responsible for the words. This time, he writes to the church at Corinth. Paul teaches them many timeless truths about eternity and the end times in this book. In 2 Corinthians 4:16–17 (KJV), he shares this powerful message.

For which cause we faint not; but though our outward man perish, yet the inward man is renewed day by day. For our light affliction, which is but for a moment, worketh for us a far more exceeding and eternal weight of glory.

Previous to this passage Paul shares his belief that just as Jesus was raised by God, we, too, will be raised, and this gospel of grace is reaching more and more people. Many people were being transformed by the message and many were, therefore, going to be in heaven. He finishes his point by saying that for this cause, we do not faint.

The reason why we do not faint is because we have an understanding. Whatever is going on with us has an internal benefit and an eternal benefit. Internally, our inward man is being renewed day by day. He, the inward man, is becoming stronger day by day. At the same time, as we are experiencing this internal benefit, there is being produced a weight of glory on our lives that will last throughout eternity.

It becomes glowing clear by reading 2 Corinthians 4:16–17 in the Message Bible. I will end the chapter with this paraphrase of the passage:

> So we're not giving up. How could we! Even though on the outside it often looks like things are falling apart on us, on the inside, where God is making new life, not a day goes by without his unfolding grace. These hard times are small potatoes compared to the coming good times, the lavish celebration prepared for us. There's far more here than meets the eye. The things we see now are here today, gone tomorrow. But the things we can't see now will last forever.

I'm Going to Get you Through This!

For the most part, I have attempted to stay true to the purpose behind this book which is to primarily provide as much practical teaching on getting through what you are going through, just in case we do not receive an instant miracle. I have dealt with this because I do not believe there is enough said about the things we have to go through in life. When we do not know how to respond to the things we have to go through, then we may bring dishonor to the kingdom by acting in an ungodly way or losing our faith in our God.

We have to come to grips with the fact that some people are chosen, out of God's sovereignty, to go through adverse things. As a pastor, I have watched faith-filled people in my ministry deal with debilitating sicknesses, and we prayed for healing to happen for them. It did not. I can only surmise that God allowed them to go through it. I am thoroughly convinced that God could have healed them at any time. He did not.

Yet most of these people left the earth with tremendous applause by those left behind because they never gave up faith, they never stopped honoring Christ, and they never stopped living although they were dying. I believe God was pleased and glorified even in what we may not understand.

Before I close this book, however, I wanted to tell you what I believe. I believe in miracles. I believe we should believe in miracles until there is no reason to believe. I have not discovered the scriptures many say exist to prove miracles no longer exist. Therefore, since I believe in miracles, let me say to you, you are going to get through whatever you are going through. Yep, I said it, and I will say it again, you will get through whatever you are going through. You will get through it because God will deliver you.

The Bible is full of examples of God being a deliverer. He delivered the children of Israel from Egypt and through the Red Sea. He delivered Daniel from a lion's den. He delivered Esther and the Jews from extinction by the hand of the Persians. He delivered David from the delusional attempts of King Saul to take his life. He delivered Paul and Silas at midnight from an inner most prison. Likewise, he delivered Peter from jail as the church gathered in a home to pray for his emancipation. God delivered Paul from shipwrecks and a snake bite. Most impressively of all, God delivered the lifeless Jesus from a tomb in which He had been laid for three days.

Our entire Gospel message hangs on this deliverance. We must believe it in order to be a child of God.

Recalling God's impressive deliverance record should allow you to believe God will deliver you. The Bible says we are afflicted by many things, but God delivers us from them all. It is imperative for you to confess, "I am going to get through this!" Sure, it may be tough now. It may feel like there is no way out now. Nonetheless, you have to rise up in your faith and believe and declare, "I am going to get through this!"

Deliverance is on the other side of your confession. When we come to the place where we agree with the promises of God's Word, then those promises manifest in our lives. There is no promise God gives that He is not capable of performing.

I have seen God's work, and because I have seen God's work, I could not finish this book without telling you that as you read this, "You are a candidate for a miracle." If you have settled in your mind to just accept your plight as your ordinary way of life, I want to change your mind-set. This book was never meant for you to settle, it was meant to help you to cope until the miracle, blessing, breakthrough, or will of God comes.

Peter and John run into a settler one day. It is a lame man who is laid at the temple every day to ask for alms. As the Apostles approach, the lame man does what he has always done, expects to receive what he always receives. He asks Peter and John for some cash, not knowing that this is the day he is going to get something more valuable than money. His miracle is about to take place.

Peter makes one of the most famous statements recorded in the New Testament to the lame man. Looking at him, he says, "Silver and gold, have I none. But such as I have, I give unto thee. In the name of Jesus Christ of Nazareth, rise up and walk."

What happens next is amazing. Peter takes the lame man by the hand and immediately his feet and ankle bones receive strength. He gets up leaping and praising God.

I pray today is the day you receive this level of strength—the strength to do what you could not do before and the strength to overcome your limitation, your burden, or your pain. I pray this strength changes you. I pray strength to your body, your internal organs, your mind, your will, and to your spirit. God, my friend, has not forgotten about you. You will make it through. You will experience victory.

Recently, I shared some insight concerning Abraham with some students I was teaching in Bible college. I showed them how the Bible illuminates Abraham's faith when he had to believe God was going to bring a child through him and Sarah. Abraham's faith is the kind of faith we all should aspire. First, let's look at the scriptures:

> Who against hope believed in hope, that he might become the father of many nations, according to that which was spoken, So shall thy seed be. And being not weak in faith, he considered not his own body now dead, when he was about an hundred years old, neither yet the deadness of Sarah's womb: He staggered not at the promise of God through unbelief; but was strong in faith, giving glory to God; And being fully persuaded that, what he had promised, he was able also to perform. (Romans 4:18–21, KJV)

There are five essentials of Abraham's faith. We are going to use these essentials to get to our place of victory. First, he believed when there was no reason to believe. The text said, "Against hope, he believed in hope." There was no tangible evidence to believe, yet he did. Secondly, his faith did not weaken; and thirdly, his faith did not waiver. And the final two things we see here is Abraham was strong in the faith, and he was fully convinced of God's ability.

Let these words speak of you. God is able. He can and He will.

About the Author

E rnest W. Jones has served True Vine Ministries church as senior pastor from its beginning in 1992 with six members to its 1,500 members today. He has earned doctorate degrees in pastoral and Christian counseling and an MA in church history. He also serves as dean of the Family Bible College of Fayetteville in Fayetteville, North Carolina. Ernest and his wife, Cynthia, have been married since 1984 and have one child, Jessica, from their union.

CPSIA information can be obtained
at www.ICGtesting.com
Printed in the USA
JSHW020443251019
2050JS00003B/2